Wilderness in NEPAL

Lydia Paton, Fiona Paton and Tom Giles

All proceeds from the sale of this book
will be donated to the Bhadure School and
the Kushudebu Public Health Mission in Nepal.

© for the collection held by Wilderness School
© for photographs held by individual photographers

Wilderness School
30 Hawkers Road
Medindie
SA 5081
www.wilderness.com.au

First published in Australia 2008 by Wilderness School

National Library of Australia Cataloguing-in-Publication entry

Author: Paton, Lydia Jean, 1983-

Title: Wilderness in Nepal / Lydia Paton, Tom Giles, Fiona Paton.

Edition: 1st ed.

ISBN: 978 0 9596156 5 4 (hbk.)

Subjects: Nepal--Description and travel.

Other Authors/Contributors:
                 Giles, Thomas O'Halloran, 1951-
                 Paton, Fiona Laura, 1986-

Dewey Number: 915.426

Graphic Design: Cogdell Design & Fine Art   www.graemecogdell.com.au

Printing: Hyde Park Press   www.hydeparkpress.com.au

Cover photo 1

Foreword

IN 1998 BRONWEN MARTIN, the visionary force behind the trips to Nepal, led the first of the many treks that Wilderness School has undertaken. Dr Sally Nobbs, with her dedication and motivation, has continued these wonderful adventures for the girls and the wider Wilderness community. For the last 10 years the Wilderness community has been trying to make a difference.

The Daleki School in Kathmandu was the first school supported by Wilderness. The Daleki School had plans to establish another school in a rural area outside Kathmandu. This however became more difficult after the King was assassinated and the Nepalese Government no longer would guarantee money. The school was also difficult for Wilderness trekkers to visit, so this plan did not eventuate.

Wilderness continued to look for a rural school to support, and received a letter from the headmaster of the Bhadure School with the following statement:

> 'Father is 33 years old and Mother is 30 years old they have five children, two daughters 11 and 3 and three sons 9,7 and 5. They live in a poor rural area of Nepal. The father and mother are working as labourers and tenant farmers and earn 800 rupees (approximately $40) a month. Mother is also working as a housewife. None of the children go to school because of poverty and unawareness. They just go to catch rats and play on the road. Mother sometimes goes to collect firewood'.

Thus the connection to the Bhadure School was established and they have been given a guarantee of long term financial support.

When I visited the Bhadure School, our group was escorted by a wonderful musical procession with singing and dancing. We were warmly welcomed to the school with garlands of flowers and blessings of red face dust. The entire school was there to greet us; children, teachers, their families and villagers. Before Bhadure School was built these children had to walk many kilometres to get to their previous school. A tragedy of a little boy drowning on his way to school in another village during the monsoon season prompted the villagers to establish Bhadure School.

Wilderness also supports the Child Haven Orphanage in Kathmandu, supplying clothing and books.

In the Beni District, a very isolated area of the Everest Region high in the Himalayas, we have helped establish a medical centre. This had been a dream of Ang Tshering Sherpa, a leader of one of the previous expeditions and, with help from Wilderness School, this has now become a reality.

On another trip I witnessed the enthusiasm of the people of the Beni District in welcoming us all to the village - trekkers from Wilderness, doctors from Kathmandu and a local film crew.

A concert and blessing preceded an open clinic for the many hundreds who had walked to the village, some taking two days to get there from their homes.

Nepal and its people are beautiful, both physically and spiritually, and their calmness and serenity is humbling.

The porters make it easy for us to enjoy the beauty of Nepal. We trek, puff and pant and struggle to carry our small backpacks with our up to date trekking gear. They, on the other hand, walk happily along in thongs and 'hand me down clothes' laughing and joking with us while carrying our duffel bags, tents, cooking gear, toilet tent and the occasional live chicken.

The scenery is breathtaking – mountain peaks rise above villages, paths meander between the houses and bridges cross raging rivers.

So far the Wilderness community has raised $72,000 through such activities as a Big Lunch, Big Night In and the sale of pashminas, beanies and jewellery, all of which have been brought from Nepal. The shaving of Dr Sally Nobbs' head raised a spectacular $3000 and in 2006 a very successful dinner raised over $38,000.

I hope this book will inspire you to reach out to the Nepalese people and help us to help them.

K. M. Harbison

Kathy Harbison
Lady Mayoress of Adelaide
April 2008

Photo 2

This book is dedicated to Dr Sally Nobbs
in her tireless efforts for fundraising for the people of Nepal.

Contents

Scale

0   50   100 mi
0   50   100   150 km

CHINA

GREAT HIMALAYA RANGE

NEPAL

Simikot
Namja Pass
Dandeldhura
Ridikot
Silgarhi
SHEY-PHOKSUMDO NATIONAL PARK
Mustang
Mahendranagar
Dailekh
Dhangarhi
Birendranagar
Jajarkot
Dhavlagiri 8167
Annapurna 8081
Manaslu 8163
Cho Oyu 8201
Mount Everest 8848
Makalu I 8463
Kanchenjunga 8586
ROYAL BARDIA WILDLIFE RESERVE
MAHABHARAT RANGE
SIWALIK
Sallyan
Bhadure
Baglung
Pokhara
Kusma
LANGTANG NATIONAL PARK
Pyuthan
Gorkha
Tulsipur
Nepalganj
INDIA
Tansen
KATHMANDU VALLEY
Butwal
Kathmandu
Bhaktpur
Taulihawa
Bhairahawa
Patan
Banepa
Junbesi
Bharatpur
Lumbini
ROYAL CHITWAN NATIONAL PARK
Hitaura
Amlekhgani
Taplejung
BHUTAN
PARSA WILDLIFE RESERVE
Kalaiya
Binaipur
Dhankuta
Ilam
INDIA
SIWALIK RANGE
MAHABHARAT RANGE
Janakpur
Lahan
Dharan
Jalesvar
Raibirai
Biratnagar
Bhadepur

BANGLADESH

Nuptse 7861
Everest 8848
Lhotse 8516
Everest Base Camp
Kala Paltar
Goran Shep
Lobuche East 6127
Lobuche
Dingboche
Ama Dablam 6812
Mingbo
Ama Dablam Base Camp 5200
Phortse
Khumjung
Tengboche
Namche Bazaar
Monjo
Phakding
Lukla
EVEREST REGION TREKKING MAP
NOT TO SCALE
Painyea
Nunphala
Junbesi
Khanikholav
Phaplu

Dhaulagiri 8167
Annapurna I 8081
Khopra Ridge 4100
Huin Chuli 6441
Chistibung
Chitri
Do Bado
Machupuchare Base Camp 4100
Poon Hill 3210
Gorepani
Tadopani
Ghandruk
Ramche
Ulleri
Lespar
Sauli Bazaar
Landruk
Australia Camp
Birenthani
Serangot
Naya Pul
Bhadure
Phewa Lake
Pokhara
ANNAPURNA REGION TREKKING MAP
NOT TO SCALE
Panchese Peak
Benkar

Kathmandu

*"I love Kathmandu,
where legends worthy of the
Thousand and One Nights
overlap with history, and the
Middle Ages still linger, gently
resisting the advances of the
modern world."*

- Pierre Toutain

KATHMANDU IS THE CAPITAL, largest city and cultural heart of the Kingdom of Nepal, the tiny Himalayan country pocketed between Tibet and India. The city itself is built within the Kathmandu Valley, and is home to over one million people. It has a rich history, evidence of which can be seen almost immediately upon arrival at the International Airport, only six kilometres out of the city. Civilization in the valley dates from 185 AD, when the Kirats became the first documented rulers; the remains of their palace can be found nearby. The oldest building is 1,992 years old, a remarkable feat considering the region is particularly earthquake prone.

But despite its far-reaching heritage, the modern Kathmandu is a mosaic of cultures and peoples that reflects its unique position at the crossroads of cultures between Asia and the Indian sub-continent; bustling markets and streets overflowing with commotion collide daily with centuries old palaces, temples, and monasteries. Kathmandu is an intoxicating mix of the old and the new, and this fresh combination is not lost on most travellers. There is at once an air of youthful celebration and a deep reverence for history which invites visitors to explore further this "huge, ancient, but living museum."

Kathmandu today is a tourist hub, a testament not only to the remarkable attraction of the Himalayas but also to the vibrancy of the city itself. It has been a key stop on the hippie itinerary since the 1960s, and has inspired songs from Cat Stevens, Bob Seger, and many others. The well-known Thamel district is an intricate network of crowded markets and street vendors, where it is possible to purchase delicate silk skirts, goat heads, and handmade Buddhist statues in one fell swoop. Durbar Square is also a popular destination for travellers; it dissects the three main cities which make up the Kathmandu Valley – Kathmandu, Patan, and Bhaktapur – and is the sight of many of the region's revered temples. The city serves as a pilgrimage destination for both Buddhists and Hindus, although the overall impression of Kathmandu is one of religious tolerance and diversity, where multiple faiths and belief systems intertwine to create a lively and pluralistic society that most find utterly absorbing.

Like many of the world's large metropolises, Kathmandu suffers from its fair share of problems. These range from pollution, a serious risk to many of the precious monuments it has become so famous for, to the overcrowding and poor living conditions of its inhabitants. However, one cannot help but become entirely immersed in the energy and spirit of Kathmandu, which was named as a UNESCO World Heritage Site in 1979. There is something to suit everyone in this melting pot of cultures, traditions, beliefs and backgrounds. It is very hard to come away disappointed.

Athena Taylor, Wilderness School Student

Photo 3 (previous page)
Photo 4 (opposite)

"Kathmandu has a population of 1.2 million
and the valley is crowded and smoggy."

Photo 7

"Apparently one should ask their price and then halve it.
It is hard to understand how so many tiny shops survive because
you rarely see Nepalese people buying anything."

Photo 8

KATHMANDU **17**

Photo 9 (above)
Photo 10 (opposite)

"Boudhanath is the biggest Buddhist stupa in the world
and the oldest in Nepal."

Photo 13
Photo 14 (OPPOSITE PAGE)

"They mix
the paints for
the Mandela
themselves and
use 24ct gold
to make the
gold paint."

PHOTO 15
PHOTO 16 (OPPOSITE PAGE)

24   KATHMANDU

Photo 20

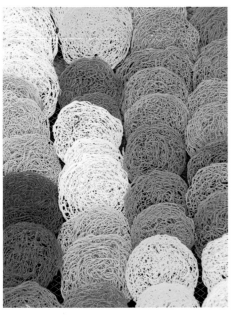

Photo 21 (top)
Photo 22 (bottom left)
Photo 23 (bottom right)
Photo 24 (opposite page)

Photo 25

"From the window of our bus we saw butchers' shops, idle people,
women doing their laundry in the streets, sleeping dogs and
people collecting drinking water."

Photo 27

Photo 28 (top left)
Photo 29 (top right)
Photo 30 (bottom right)

"After the cremation
the ashes are pushed
into the river and other
people wash in it because
it is holy water."

Photo 31 (TOP)
Photo 32 (BOTTOM)

PHOTO 33

Photo 34 (top)
Photo 35 (bottom)

"The best present I ever received was a chicken from my grandmother.
She gave it to me so I could sell the eggs to buy pens for school."
Ang Sherpa

Photo 37 (TOP LEFT)
Photo 38 (RIGHT)
Photo 39 (BOTTOM LEFT)

PHOTO 40
PHOTO 41 (NEXT PAGE)

"We visited the Child Haven Orphanage
where the children did a traditional dance for us. Afterwards we taught
them how to do the hokey-pokey."

Pokhara

> "The entire valley is a marvellous region, with beauty and culture aplenty for anybody willing to explore."

THE SLOW BOAT RIDE across Pokhara's immense Phewa Lake can hardly fade from the traveller's memory; a 4.4 sq km lake at 800 metres above sea level, it shimmers with the reflection of the steep forested hills that hem the lake on all sides. Its glassy surface, dotted sporadically with the boats of weathered fishermen, is a quiet escape after the chaos of Pokhara's bustling streets.

The second largest town in Nepal, Pokhara lies on what was once an important trading route between Tibet and India. Even to this day the mix of cultures created by this intermingling remains visible, with a number of ancient buildings offering clear evidence of cultural variety. After the annexation of Tibet in 1959, over 300,000 Tibetan refugees fled and settled in Nepal, many of them in the Pokhara valley; as a result, Tibetan influence in the region is very strong.

Until the 1960s, Pokhara was only accessible by foot, which added further mystery to an already magical destination. Today, thanks to an airport and extensive improvement of Nepal's roads, it attracts thousands of international visitors each year, who use the town as a starting point for many of the treks into the Himalayas. Whether embarking on a short and leisurely trip into the nearby jungle or a challenging ascent of Annapurna's many daunting summits, travellers will find Pokhara a perfect starting point. The city itself is picturesque and has benefited extensively from the revenue generated by tourists. They have provided locals with jobs as guides and porters, as well as a stream of interested customers for the stalls which line most of Pokhara's main streets, their colourful windows adorned with everything from sweets to batteries, rusted coke bottles to postcards.

Merely a few hours walking can direct a curious trekker deep into the dense jungle, or to the site of the World Peace Pagoda, one of eighty Buddhist Stupas designed to provide a harmonious focus for people of all races and creeds and which provides an inspiring view of central Pokhara, as well as the Annapurna Range. The site is a place of reflective meditation, lined with Buddhist prayer flags and impenetrable foliage. Add to this the mountains shimmering in the distance, and it becomes a vital stop on the traveller's journey through Nepal.

Not only does Pokhara offer an insight into the vibrant city life of the Nepalese people, but also into the natural wonders situated so close to this human commotion. The entire valley is a marvellous region, with beauty and culture aplenty for anybody willing to explore.

Athena Taylor, Wilderness School Student

PHOTO 42 (PREVIOUS PAGE)
PHOTO 43 (OPPOSITE)

Photo 44

"We spent our first night under canvas by the Pokhara lake. As we gazed around us at the mountains we would climb we were told by our guide, Ramesh, that the next day would involve a little bit up and a little bit down. We soon realised that the Nepalese interpretation of 'a little bit' is very different from ours."

Photo 45

"Pokhara is beautifully situated on the banks of Phewa Lake
and nowhere else in the world do mountains rise so steeply.
Within 30 kilometres of the city the elevation changes by 7000 metres."

PHOTO 52

Photo 53
Photo 54 (opposite)

Annapurna

THE HIMALAYAN MOUNTAIN RANGE can be found on the front of any travel brochure featuring Nepal. It is by far the most prominent tourist attraction of the country, an immense and infinitely beautiful mountain system which separates the Indian sub-continent from the Tibetan Plateau. Of this vast geographical wonder, perhaps one of the best known destinations for visitors is Annapurna. The Annapurna region consists of a series of peaks in central Nepal, stretching over 55 kilometres through some of the most magnificent settings on Earth. Its highest mountain, Annapurna I, is ranked tenth in the world and part of the 14 "eight-thousanders". The most dramatic peak, on the other hand, is the pyramidal Machapuchare, the sacred mountain, which can be aptly translated as "fishtail" and lies just 30 kilometres from Pokhara, the area's largest town. Annapurna itself means Goddess of Fertility in Sanskrit and represents the goddess of fertility and agriculture in the Hindu religion.

There are three main routes through central Nepal: to Jomsom and Muktinath, to Annapurna Sanctuary, and a circuit of the Annapurna Himal itself. The landscape offers a wide variety of breath-taking mountain peaks, terraced villages, and old-growth forests that in a single trek can transform from dark woods of rhododendrons, to steamy jungles filled with the chattering of monkeys. The gentle grazing and farming land of small rural towns can change within a matter of hours into a dense assortment of teeming forest life before that too gives way to a thundering waterfall; with more ascension it is possible to leave all this behind and find oneself nestled within the clouds. The diversity of the scenery is truly breathtaking.

Dotted throughout this marvellous terrain, which attracts over two thirds of the country's trekkers, are a multitude of quaint hotels which sit comfortably alongside the ancient cultural and religious sites of the local Nepali people. The region's culture stems from its peoples, whose ancestral origins and vast array of religions add a human touch to the often surreal experience of trekking through Annapurna. The multitude of beliefs of the many ethnic groups which inhabit the heartland of Nepal mix with relative ease, and serve as an example to the observant traveller of the tolerance that is possible when differences are cherished and respected. The Nepali people themselves are friendly, curious and wholeheartedly hospitable, with a sincerity and warmth that rarely fails to elicit a smile.

Today, serious environmental concerns exist throughout the Annapurna region about the speed of deforestation. Trees are disappearing at an alarming rate to build lodges and supply firewood for hot water and cooking. If deforestation continues at such a pace much of the glorious environmental variety could be lost. However, positive action is being taken; the Annapurna Conservation Area Project, the largest in Nepal, aims to combine environmental protection with sustainable community development. Central to its ideals is the use of alternative energy sources and the translation of tourism into a higher standard of living for the Nepali people. This initiative is now firmly embedded and, with the support of environmentally conscious trekkers, the benefits of sustainability are beginning to be realised.

Athena Taylor, Wilderness School Student

"One of the amazing things about the trek was the constant variation in the environments through which we walked. These ranged from rhododendron forests, alpine plains and steep rocky tracks to walking through rice fields and villages with terraced cornfields."

"Up or down
often involves
thousands of steps;
short distances as
the crow flies, but
much greater when
one takes contours
into account."

Photo 58

58   A N N A P U R N A

Photo 59

Photo 60
Photo 61 (opposite page)

"My calves are killing me and I think tomorrow
they will be even tighter than they were this morning."

Photo 62

Photo 63 (top left)
Photo 64 (top right)
Photo 65 (bottom)

PHOTO 66 (TOP LEFT)
PHOTO 67 (RIGHT)
PHOTO 68 (BOTTOM LEFT)

Photo 69

Photo 72

"We crossed a bridge made from rotten timber which was held together with stones. It seemed dodgy but a couple of cows crossed first so it must have held some considerable weight."

Photo 73

Photo 74

ANNAPURNA   69

PHOTO 75 (LEFT)
PHOTO 76 (RIGHT)

"We camped alongside a little
village called Pothana and in the
evening the fog settled a little and
we could see the cap
of Annapurna I."

Photo 77

PHOTO 78

Photo 79

"After lunch Adrian tried to carry part of the kitchen on his head
- needless to say we nearly lost the kitchen."

Photo 80 (left)
Photo 81 (right)

Photo 82

Photo 83

Photo 84

Photo 85

78 ANNAPURNA

Photo 86

"The view of
Annapurna South
was out of this world.
These mountains
look extremely high,
dangerous and
liberally covered in
snow – very beautiful!"

"Our sherpas are happy with the group's reactions to their picturesque country."

Photo 87 (top)
Photo 88 (bottom)

80   ANNAPURNA

Photo 89

Photo 90
Photo 91 (opposite)

"A constant highlight was our interaction with our Nepalese sherpas, who had great patience and good humour when members of the group felt daunted by the physical exertion demanded of them."

Photo 92

"Sherpa guides earn 180 rupees a day which is equivalent to $3.60."

Photo 93

WE ARE FIGHTING FOR ~~THE~~ THE RIGHT OF THE COMMON PEOPLE

जिन्दावाद

Photo 94

"Had been looking forward to calling home from Ghandruk,
but Maoists have taken the telephones
and pulled the lines down."

Photo 95 (top)
Photo 96 (bottom left)
Photo 97 (bottom right)

Photo 98

Photo 99

ANNAPURNA 89

"The people living
up here seem
to have a much
higher quality of
life. The chickens,
cows, dogs and
buffalo seem
healthier and the
water is much
cleaner because
it comes straight
from the melting
snow."

Photo 100

Photo 106

Photo 111

Photo 112

100 ANNAPURNA

PHOTO 115

"We walked through rhododendron forests – although not in flower –
still quite beautiful and fairytale like."

"The river at the bottom was a grey raging torrent. We found a pool to one side in which we could wash our clothes, bodies and hair. It was very cold but eased the ache in our muscles."

Photo 116

103

Photo 117

Photo 118

Photo 119

Photo 130

"After a few days of trekking, we came to Bhadure and the school we sponsor. We were greeted with garlands of flowers, blessings of red face dust and buffalo milk."

Photo 131 (top)
Photo 132 (bottom)
Photo 133 (opposite page)

Photo 134

Photo 140 (left)
Photo 141 (right)

Photo 142 (top left)
Photo 143 (top right)
Photo 144 (bottom)
Photo 145 (opposite page)

Photo 146

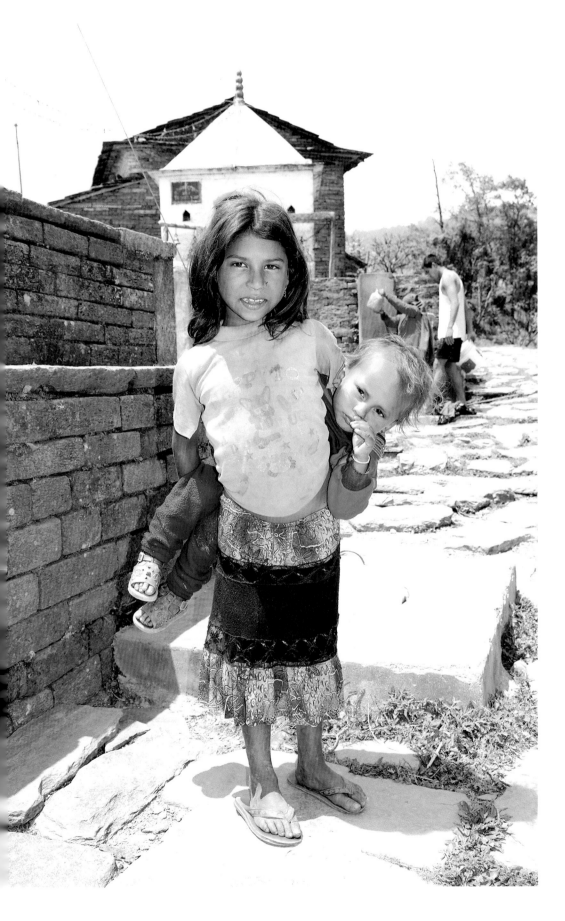

Photo 147 (LEFT)
Photo 148 (TOP RIGHT)
Photo 149 (BOTTOM RIGHT)

"When the headmaster spoke, a personal highlight of his welcome was the phrase "Our happiness knows no boundaries.""

PHOTO 150

"Namasté –
I salute the divine
within you."

Photo 151

ANNAPURNA **129**

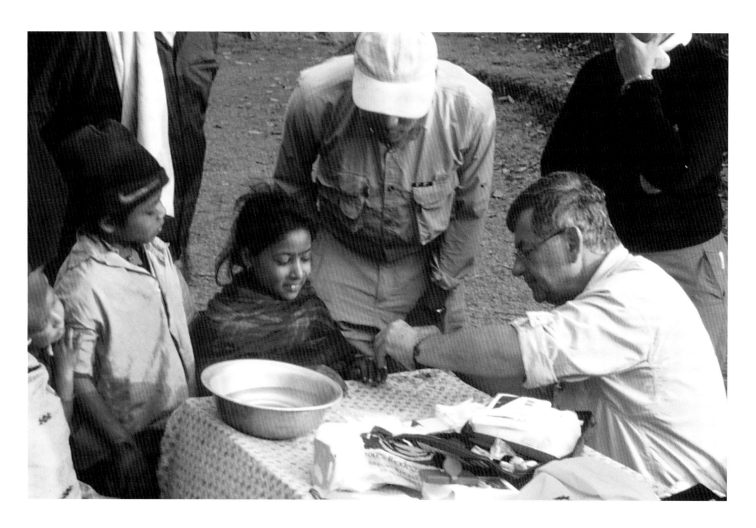

"Adrian carried a medical kit and frequently treated children's wounds and infections."

Photo 152 (top)
Photo153 (bottom)
Photo 154 (opposite page)

Photo 155

132 ANNAPURNA

Photo 156 (left)
Photo 157 (right)

PHOTO 158

Photo 166

Photo 167

140 ANNAPURNA

141

Photo 169
Photo 170 (opposite page)

142

Chitwan

PHOTO 174 (LEFT)
PHOTO 175 (RIGHT)

"In one day an elephant eats
200 kilograms of greens and
100 elephant cookies."

"Here a baby elephant demonstrates how strong and
clumsy it is at 37 days old."

"The Royal Chitwan National Park is a haven for many animals, including the Indian Elephant, Bengal Tiger and the Greater One-Horned Rhinoceros."

PHOTO 177 (TOP)
PHOTO 178 (OPPOSITE PAGE)

150   CHITWAN

Everest

AS THE HIGHEST PEAK on the Earth's surface, Mount Everest is an awe-inspiring destination. Stretching a phenomenal 8,848 metres into the air, it is a landmark visible from space and which, for many at least, represents the pinnacle of adventurous climbing. Even seen from a distance, Everest is enough to take one's breath away, whether its peak is shrouded in snow clouds or glistening in the bright light of morning.

Although it is in essence just over 200 metres higher than its closest rival, Mount Everest represents the epicentre of the mountaineering world, drawing the efforts of hundreds of climbers each year, as well as thousands more to the South and North base camps. As a result, it has become a major contributor to Nepal's economy, with the government requiring all prospective climbers to purchase an expensive $US25,000 permit.

But it is not just the mountain which attracts international prominence. High in the mountains surrounding Everest is the traditional homeland of the legendary Sherpa people, who have won global renown for their ability and indomitable will in scaling the most formidable peaks on the planet. Ironically, the Sherpa people did not climb mountains before the arrival of Westerners, considering them the sacred and reverential homes of the Gods. This attitude has changed, however, with the economic opportunities that mountain climbing offers. Today the Sherpa people hold many impressive Everest records, including the most times summitted for men and women, the quickest ascent and descent, the most time spent on top and the youngest climber to reach the summit. Mountaineering is now inherently part of the Sherpa culture.

The people themselves share many similarities with Tibetan culture, having migrated from Eastern Tibet hundreds of years ago. They are Buddhists and their language, literature, history and philosophy all have their origins in Tibet. Despite the influences of foreigners and increased financial opportunity, the ancient customs of the Sherpas have been preserved. Rather than having a detrimental effect on the Everest Region, Westerners now play a crucial role in supporting and maintaining Sherpa traditions.

This beautiful and entrancing area of Nepal is no longer an untouched paradise; the path to the summit is littered with empty oxygen bottles, aluminum cans, various forms of plastic, glass, clothes, climbing equipment, paper, food and even dead bodies. Much of the waste is non-biodegradable and that which is, often does not break down due to the extreme conditions, prompting some conservationists to label Everest the highest junkyard in the world. Attempts are now being made to clean the mountain, such as making trips for the purpose of collecting rubbish. With a new government in Nepal, environmentalists are hopeful that further action will be taken to preserve the Everest region and its spectacular beauty for generations to come.

Athena Taylor, Wilderness School Student

Photo 179 (OPPOSITE)

PHOTO 183

Photo 184

"Lung-ta prayer flags are hung in places where the wind will catch them."

Photo 185

158 EVEREST

Photo 190

"In Nepal white yaks are very expensive and rare, selling for around four thousand Australian dollars."

"An incredible view from Kala Pattar - the Khumbu Icefall
with Nuptse and Mt Everest in the background."

"Our camp for tonight
is the stoned-off area of
a Yak's quarters –
complete with Yak and
baby Yaktung."

Photo 196

EVEREST **167**

Photo 197 (top)
Photo 198 (bottom)

Photo 199

Photo 200

170 EVEREST

Photo 201

Photo 202 (left)
Photo 203 (right)

"The colours of the prayer flags symbolise various elements
and are hung in a specific order: blue (sky/space), white (air/wind),
red (fire), green (water) and finally yellow (earth)."

Photo 204 (left))
Photo 205 (right)

"The morning was bitterly cold
and everyone rugged up
for the walk."

Photo 206

Photo 207 (top)
Photo 208 (bottom)

"At the top of
Thokla Pass
there were many
memorials to the
trekkers who died
trying to climb
Everest."

Photo 209

Photo 210

Photo 211

Photo 212

Photo 213 (top)
Photo 214 (bottom)

Photo 215

"Everything for the building of the Kushudebu Public Health Mission
is carried to Junbesi by porters."

PHOTO 216

182 EVEREST

PHOTO 217 (TOP)
PHOTO 218 (BOTTOM)

Photo 219

"Some patients have
walked for five days
to receive treatment."

PHOTO 220 (TOP)
PHOTO 221 (BOTTOM)

"Namasté is a commonly used greeting in Nepal and expresses deep respect for another — it is often accompanied by hands folded in a prayer position."

Photo 222 (top)
Photo 223 (bottom)

186   EVEREST

PHOTO 224 (TOP)
PHOTO 225 (BOTTOM LEFT)
PHOTO 226 (BOTTOM RIGHT)

PHOTO 227

Kushudebu Public Health Mission

THE DECISION TO HELP the Junbesi community in their dream to build a clinic for their people came about during the 2005 Community trek. Ang Tshering Sherpa, the leader of the expedition, so inspired members of the trek that they returned home and began fundraising for the project.

The Kushudebu Public Health Mission has been a huge success and after more than two years of operation has become a vital service for the surrounding rural community. Its objectives are to improve the health of the orphaned and disadvantaged in the region, as well as to promote a better understanding of good health practices to reduce the rate of premature and preventable death. Health care has now been provided to over 2000 people, some of whom must walk five days to receive treatment. Further improvements are planned for the near future, such as carrying a 750 kilogram X-ray machine from the nearest airport to the Health Mission, a journey that will take over five days to complete.

During the past ten years, over $72,000 has been raised by the Wilderness School community for important projects in Nepal. This money has been raised by the students' efforts and a fundraising dinner held in 2006. Of this money, $17,000 has been donated to the medical centre so far. This contribution was recognised when over one thousand villagers attended a welcoming ceremony in Junbesi for eight members of the 2007 Community trek. In addition, the school's symbol, the lion rampant, was carried to the summit of Mount Everest by Ang's brother to be placed at the top of the world, alongside the flags of the seven political parties of Nepal and Amnesty International.

What often seems a fundamental right in our society - hospital beds or stretchers and casts with which to fix a broken bone - can mean all the difference in Nepal between a swift recovery and permanent injury, or even death. Wilderness School understands the significance of the Health Mission and the difference it has made to the lives of the Junbesi villagers and surrounding rural families. We pledge to continue our support for the medical centre and hope that this book will inspire and encourage more people to do the same. If we follow the belief that 'from little things, big things grow', then who knows what we can achieve in Nepal in the future?

Athena Taylor, Wilderness School Student

PHOTO 228: ASSEMBLING THE X-RAY MACHINE.

PHOTO 229: ANG SHERPA

Bhadure School

NESTLED IN THE MOUNTAINS of western Nepal, 35 kilometres out of Pokhara, is the small rural village of Bhadure. At nearly 2000 metres above sea level, the town is encompassed by picturesque mountains, with the Annapurna Range an awe-inspiring backdrop to the quiet serenity of the forests. The village consists of loosely grouped homes made predominantly from mud-brick, stone, bamboo or wood, with thatch, slate or tin roofs. The main occupation of the local people is agriculture, as well as shop keeping and teaching at the local school. The people of Bhadure fit into seven castes but, despite this, the thousand strong population has a sound sense of community and friendship.

There are 280 families and over 300 children serviced by Bhadure School, which offers pre-primary education through to grade 10. The school employs 14 teachers, with nine sponsored by the Nepali Government and an additional five paid at the local level. The cost of these extra teachers is estimated at 30,000 NRS ($AU512) per month and since 2006, Wilderness School has allocated $AU5000 per year to help pay these salaries.

Bhadure School has many needs, including replacing old, damaged buildings, constructing toilets for the children, acquiring another 50 desks, plastering the walls of the classrooms, fitting the windows with glass and building a new room for pre-primary classes. Currently, with the funding provided by Wilderness School, Bhadure School is tackling these needs.

The school's resources are rudimentary; most children have few, if any, school supplies and rely on little more than a blackboard and chalk to guide them through their education. Textbooks, paper, pens and computers are unheard of luxuries for the children of Bhadure. Despite this, the school gives children a much greater chance of attending university and forging better lives for themselves and their communities. According to the Headmaster of Bhadure, Ramprasad Poudel, the positive effects of this education are already being seen around the village: "Parents who cannot even afford sandals for their feet are seeing their children go to school and have the opportunity to study at university. This has been a great relief during a difficult time in Nepal." The first two students to pass their SLC (school level certificate) were Som Prasad Gurung and Salik Ram Poudel, who have both been accepted into university.

There is a hunger in the community of Bhadure to give their young the best possible start in the world, and bestow upon them the skills necessary to improve their lives and create a better future. With the continuing assistance of the Wilderness community and the dedication of the villagers in their support of the school, this dream is being realised. The future, for Bhadure's children at least, looks bright.

Athena Taylor, Wilderness School Student